D0368542

One-Minute
PRAYERS™
✦ ✦ ✦ ✦ ✦
to Begin and End Your Day

Text by Hope Lyda

HARVEST HOUSE PUBLISHERS
EUGENE, OREGON

ONE-MINUTE PRAYERS is a series trademark of The Hawkins Children's LLC. Harvest House Publishers, Inc., is the exclusive licensee of the trademark ONE-MINUTE PRAYERS.

The text is taken from *One-Minute Prayers™ to Start Your Day* and *One-Minute Prayers™ to End Your Day.*

Cover photo © David Loftus / Riser / Getty Images

Cover by Franke Design and Illustration, Minneapolis, Minnesota

ONE-MINUTE PRAYERS™ TO BEGIN AND END YOUR DAY
Copyright © 2008 by Harvest House Publishers
Published by Harvest House Publishers
Eugene, Oregon 97402
www.harvesthousepublishers.com

ISBN 978-0-7369-2104-6 (padded hardcover)

Printed in China

15 16 17 18 19   / RDS-SK / 17 16 15 14 13 12

Contents

Prayers to End Your Day

One-
Minute
Prayers™

to Begin
Your Day

Awake, My Soul

My heart is steadfast, O God,
my heart is steadfast;
I will sing and make music.
Awake, my soul!
Awake, harp and lyre!
I will awaken the dawn.

PSALM 57:7-8

Let the day dawn with music and celebration. I want to be a part of this rejoicing, Lord. You give my spirit cause for joy. Let my thoughts quickly turn to the blessings in my life so that my day begins with gratitude. Keep me from an attitude of defeat or mourning when I have been given this gift of another day.

Every minute is Yours. Please hear the music of my life. May it be pleasing to You and worthy of a new dance. Let my rejoicing bring the day from the night so that You will be praised and the world will see my light.

Beginnings

Facing the Day

At daybreak Jesus went out to a solitary place.
The people were looking for him and when they
came to where he was, they tried to keep him from
leaving them. But he said, "I must preach the good
news of the kingdom of God to the other towns
also, because that is why I was sent."

LUKE 4:42-43

God, as I face a new day, help me be mindful of what You have planned. May my focus stay on Your desires so that I do not give my time, myself, and my day to other paths or work. Grant me discernment so I can recognize when a distraction is truly an indication of Your leading and not something to avoid.

It is not easy to turn my life over, even to You. But knowing that there is a purpose for me ahead, just minutes from now and as my day unfolds, I am excited to see what today might bring.

Inviting Wisdom In

The fear of the LORD is the beginning of wisdom,
and knowledge of the Holy One is understanding.

PROVERBS 9:10

I like to act as if I know what I am doing most of the time—even when I am clueless. But Lord, this can get me into trouble. Help me seek Your wisdom and leading in more circumstances. May I begin with Your wisdom before stepping forth into this day and onto the path of my life.

My desire to know and understand my world and the people and situations in it will only be realized when I know You intimately.

A Day's Birth

I rise before dawn and cry for help; I have put my hope in your word. My eyes stay open through the watches of the night, that I may meditate on your promises.

PSALM 119:147-148

The hope I have in You is the beginning of my possibilities, my dreams, my future. Today is the beginning of the rest of my calendar of days. May I openly face all that You have for me. I wonder who You will place in my path. Will I find an open door where I least expect it? Will one step forward today be the start of something great and of Your hand?

I meditate on Your promises, Lord. They fill my heart and mind throughout the night. Now let me put my faith in those promises as a new day is born.

Giver of Life

From birth I have relied on you; you brought me forth from my mother's womb. I will ever praise you.

PSALM 71:6

When I could not yet form words that made sense to those around me…when I was unable to feed myself, walk, or consider consequences of my actions, You were my source of care and protection. You brought me into this world, and now You bring me through this life. I praise You for today. I even thank You for the trials I face. When I am misunderstood at home or at work, or I find I have made a faulty choice, I know You are here for me.

You are the One who was with me at my beginning and will be the One to embrace me at the end of my days. Thank You for Your presence and comfort every day in between.

Opportunity

Responding in Kind

Therefore, as we have opportunity, let us do good to all people, especially to those who belong to the family of believers.

GALATIANS 6:10

Soon after I called on You for grace, I turned around and was grumpy with someone who was trying to help me. I blamed this person for my day even though he was only trying to do his job. When will I learn to follow Your lead and honor all people? God, help me seek joy. Better yet, help me create joy in all circumstances.

I see today as a chance to serve others, to treat strangers and family with respect and kindness...and I see opportunities to put into practice the gift of grace in place of grumpiness, discomfort, or frustration.

Not of My Doing

The race is not to the swift or the battle to the strong, nor does food come to the wise or wealth to the brilliant or favor to the learned; but time and chance happen to them all.

ECCLESIASTES 9:11

Oh, how I would love to claim responsibility for the opportunities I have either made or taken advantage of. This would give me a sense of great accomplishment and power. But Lord, I know my good fortune is often the result of time and chance and Your goodness. I am the recipient of Your power—blessings shape my days.

When opportunity knocks, grant me the perspective and vision to see past my ego so that I understand my role was merely to turn the knob, open the door, and welcome it in. You made it, delivered it, and allowed me to recognize it.

With God

Jesus looked at them and said, "With man this is impossible, but with God all things are possible."

MATTHEW 19:26

I love to feel in control. Self-reliant. And exuding a sense of independence is a must. At least, this is what I project to the world. Truthfully—and You already know this—I depend on You for everything. Right before that meeting, I was praying for the right words and the courage to face the unknown. Before I made a decision that would impact my family, I was on my knees seeking Your will.

Lord, let me show others that You are my source of strength. Give me the confidence in You to stop keeping my weaknesses a secret. The more truth I reveal, the better I will reflect the One who makes the weak strong and the impossible possible.

Shape My Life

*But the pot he was shaping from the clay was
marred in his hands; so the potter formed it into
another pot, shaping it as seemed best to him.*

JEREMIAH 18:4

Yesterday was a bit of a bust, Lord. My big plans
withered and my high hopes tumbled. My perfect,
whole, flawless plan, once in the light of day, turned
out to have cracks galore. So here I am, facing a new
day and wanting it to be so much more. I have learned.
This day I will give over to the Potter's hands so that
You can best shape it.

I cannot wait to see what a day molded and pre-
pared by You will look like. I believe it will be strong,
beautiful, and whole.

Productivity

Seeing Your Purpose

Blessed are all who fear the LORD, who walk in his ways. You will eat the fruit of your labor; blessings and prosperity will be yours.

PSALM 128:1-2

I am in awe of You, Lord. And the more I understand Your greatness and the extent of Your power, the better able I am to give my day over to You. Help me see that to walk in Your way is the path to purpose and meaning. I want each day to count. Let the next 24 hours serve You. Move me toward my personal best to bear fruit that is pleasing to You.

Give me an understanding of productivity and purpose through Your eyes, Lord. Then when I face a detour or a distraction, I will see it for what it is—a chance to follow Your lead and be fruitful.

Giving Myself Over

Be diligent in these matters; give yourself wholly to them, so that everyone may see your progress.

1 TIMOTHY 4:15

Giver of life, grant to me passion and energy for all that I take on. Keep me bound to Your Word so that I am truthful and show integrity in all that I do. My schedule today includes difficult tasks. Help me to be diligent and mindful so others will see the work of Your hand. And when I face the projects that seem mundane, let me see their worth.

God, I want to be a contributor in all that I do. Give me strength to give every moment my very best. In my times of reflection, meditation, and prayer, may I give one hundred percent of my effort as these are offerings to You, Lord.

Legacy of Peace

*LORD, you establish peace for us; all that we have
accomplished you have done for us.*

ISAIAH 26:12

Sometimes it takes chaos for me to better understand peace. When I am in the midst of circumstances
that seem out of control or volatile, I can feel a stillness deep within that allows me to still seek You. I am
sensing Your peace. When rough times are smoothed
over and I am able to accomplish a goal, I know I have
witnessed Your peaceful protection.

You do so much for me, Lord. Without You, I am
without direction and purpose. Without You, I could
not achieve anything of eternal value. Thank You, God,
for caring for Your child.

Up to the Task

*However, I consider my life worth nothing to me,
if only I may finish the race and complete the task
the Lord Jesus has given me—the task of testifying
to the gospel of God's grace.*

ACTS 20:24

Is today the day I will learn to be an example of
Your grace, Lord? I hope so. I know that I have fallen
short in the past. I start out with good intentions, but
quickly drop them so I can reach for whatever suits
me. Money. Success. Reputation. Status. These might
reflect blessings from above, but they do little to share
Your grace with those around me.

If I want to look back upon my days with pleasure, I need to be productive as a servant, a helper, a
caregiver, a friend, and a sharer of the gospel of Your
grace.

Others

Full of Grace

Be wise in the way you act toward outsiders; make the most of every opportunity. Let your conversation be always full of grace, seasoned with salt, so that you may know how to answer everyone.

COLOSSIANS 4:5-6

Open my ears to the needs of others, Lord. Let today be my chance to really hear what is being said by those around me. Often my personal agenda fills my mind as others express their hearts. Grant me patience, openness, and compassion so I will be eager to understand others needs. Perhaps they will just need to be listened to, maybe they will need comfort, or they might need to know of Your goodness.

After listening, may I speak words that are of You and intended for that particular person. Never let my own objectives override the conversation You intend.

Righteous Way

*Do not repay anyone evil for evil. Be careful to
do what is right in the eyes of everybody. If it is
possible, as far as it depends on you, live at peace
with everyone.*

ROMANS 12:17-18

Cover me, Lord, as I go into my day. Protect me
from my own desire to be right or to have my way.
When I face someone who is not fair or just, give me
the gift of silence or wise words to diffuse the situation.
I'll admit, sometimes I would rather prove someone
wrong than prove peace is righteous.

Lead my mind to peaceful solutions. Give my heart
the tenderness it needs to see beyond evil to the needs
of the oppressed. And bless me, Lord, with the presence of mind to act in a righteous way that gives others
a glimpse of You, the Peacemaker of the soul.

Giving Out of Your Love

*If someone forces you to go one mile, go with him
two miles. Give to the one who asks you, and do
not turn away from the one who wants to borrow
from you.*

MATTHEW 5:41-42

I cannot believe how much others expect of me.
Today I will face the demands of family, coworkers,
and others who need my time. When I answer my
door, I know it will be someone who wants something
from me. Save me from my first reaction, which is to
shut down, or shut that door. Allow me to go above
and beyond what people are asking of me. You will
give me the strength and ability to do so. I need not
worry about my own shortcomings.

Today, I will come to You and ask to borrow the
patience, kindness, and love I need to go that extra
mile.

Serving the Gifts

Each one should use whatever gift he has received to serve others, faithfully administering God's grace in its various forms.

1 PETER 4:10

I love gifts! I just am not sure which ones I have, Lord. Give me Your understanding of who I am in You. Allow me to see the gifts You have built into my heart and soul so that I can use this day for good. There are moments when I see my strengths in action, but I am not always consistent. Help me see the areas in my life that should be developed. Encourage me to let go of those activities or interests that are just taking time away from what You would have me do.

I want to get the most out of this life You have given to me, Lord.

Sacrifice

Leaving It All Behind

Peter answered him, "We have left everything to follow you! What then will there be for us?"

MATTHEW 19:27

I look around me and notice the absence of some things. While some luxuries or opportunities have been excluded from my world out of preference, some have been sacrificed so that I could live a life to better serve You and those I love. I am so thankful that I came to know You and the gift of Your grace. At that time, many unnecessary trappings and circumstances fell away from my life. Now I face each day hoping that I have pared my life down to the bare essentials.

God, You do not leave me wanting for anything. So please give me the courage and insight to leave behind all that I do not need in my life.

Take This Day

I will sacrifice a freewill offering to you; I will praise your name, O LORD, for it is good.

PSALM 54:6

I pray to make this day a freewill offering to You. As I rise and begin my morning, may I consider the blessings around me so I will give You praise. May I think about the people I will interact with so that my heart will be prayerful. May I give decisions over to You so I stay within Your will and move toward Your purpose for me. May I observe the needs of others so I can serve them as Your hands.

God, this day is Yours. I give it back freely so that I might know You and Your ways better.

Acceptance Speech

When you sacrifice a thank offering to the LORD, sacrifice it in such a way that it will be accepted on your behalf.

LEVITICUS 22:29

I want to thank You, God, for providing me with a life of meaning and opportunity. When I forgot how to move through my days, You encouraged me through the kindness of others, Your Word, and glimpses of hope. Thank You for telling me the truth about Your love. You shared Your grace with my heart when I needed it most.

I wouldn't be where I am today if it weren't for You. There are many people to thank in my life, but I know the source of my understanding and my belief and inspiration is all You. Accept this heartfelt thanks—I offer You my thoughts, my work, and my praises all day long.

Change

Like a Child

And he said: "I tell you the truth, unless you change and become like little children, you will never enter the kingdom of heaven. Therefore, whoever humbles himself like this child is the greatest in the kingdom of heaven.

MATTHEW 18:3-4

How can I change my day today, Lord? In what ways do my grown-up thoughts keep me from embracing the pure, sincere faith of a child? Sometimes I think my goals hold me in a pattern of self-sufficiency, and I become unable to ask for help—even from You. My pride, my strong desire to find my own way as an adult keeps me from bowing down at Your feet and asking for Your guidance and mercy.

Show me today how to give up control and accept the changes—blessings and trials—that come with a humble, childlike faith.

Shape Me

The Spirit of the LORD will come upon you in power, and you will prophesy with them; and you will be changed into a different person.

1 SAMUEL 10:6

I give over my life to You this day. I submit my will to Your will. By releasing my agenda into Your hands, I will have the opportunity to see Your power at work in my life. Where there is resistance, grant me peace so that I can let go. Where there is doubt, grant me understanding so that I might become wise. Where there is weakness, grant me wisdom so that I might defer to Your strength.

God, every day I walk in faith should be a day to allow You to change me, shape me, and create in me the potential You planted in me.

Let Me Be Consistent

*He who is the Glory of Israel does not lie or
change his mind; for he is not a man, that he
should change his mind.*

1 SAMUEL 15:29

When I am not riding the fence with a decision, I
am often wishing I had made another choice. My feet
never seem to be on the firm ground of unwavering
faith. I question everything and everyone because of
my own faulty reasoning. God, help me focus on the
path You have for me. Let my decisions be weighed
against Your Word and will...and then let me have
peace as I move forward.

You are consistent, honest, and true. May the first
decision I make every day be to follow Your lead.

What Matters

*Command those who are rich in this present world
not to be arrogant nor to put their hope in wealth,
which is so uncertain, but to put their hope in
God, who richly provides us with everything for
our enjoyment.*

1 TIMOTHY 6:17-18

Direct me to invest my time and energy today into matters of the heart. Steer me from tagging value to temporal things of this world. You provide all that I need. When will I learn that my job is not to build an empire—my job is to serve the kingdom. It seems that I have spent a lot of my daydreams envisioning a life of status and carefree luxury when my time would be better spent imagining how I might encourage others, aid the poor, be sensitive to the wounded.

Remove my arrogance and replace it with a changed heart of humility. I will be watching for ways to place my hope in You.

Devotion

Hear My Wailing

Hezekiah turned his face to the wall and prayed to the LORD, "Remember, O LORD, how I have walked before you faithfully and with wholehearted devotion and have done what is good in your eyes." And Hezekiah wept bitterly. [And the LORD said,] "I have heard your prayer."

2 KINGS 20:2-3,5

I pray that my life is worthy of Your goodness. I value my relationship with my Creator and long to walk faithfully beside You. I have felt deep sorrow in my life, yet I have always known that You hear my cries. I pray my desire to do right and to live honorably will be pleasing to You. When my trials cause me to have doubts, may I also recall the times I cried out for help.

Remembering times of emotion inspires my devotion.

Focusing on Truth

*The works of his hands are faithful and just; all
his precepts are trustworthy. They are steadfast for
ever and ever, done in faithfulness and uprightness.*

PSALM 111:7-8

My thoughts pull me in many directions. When I
turn to Your precepts, Your truths, I become focused
and committed. I can pass through my days in a fog
until I am confronted with a situation that needs attention and prayer. This is when I step out of my routine,
my cruise-control mode, and step into my real life. I
love this time. I feel Your love, I sense Your guidance,
and I embrace Your faithfulness.

I am the work of Your hands. Forgive me when I
forget this, Lord. Return me to situations that require the
urgency of prayer and the desire to seek Your truth.

The Limitation of Need

No servant can serve two masters. Either he will hate the one and love the other, or he will be devoted to the one and despise the other. You cannot serve both God and Money.

LUKE 16:13

As I rise and face my day, I notice that my thoughts go to my financial needs. Not that I am planning major corporate takeovers, but I am dwelling on the daily ups and downs of my checking account. I feel the worry start to consume me until I can wrap my mind around a solution. I'm starting to realize how this focus takes me away from serving the One I call my Master.

Clear away this clutter. I want my waking thoughts to be devoted to You and Your priorities. I give You complete control of my financial well-being. Let me feel the freedom of this choice.

Heart and Soul

*Now devote your heart and soul to seeking the
LORD your God.*

1 CHRONICLES 22:19

From this moment on, I give my heart and soul
over to my Caretaker. You made me. You know me.
And You love me. I want to be a loyal follower who
always seeks Your face. When You shine Your grace
upon my day, it becomes a brilliant offering of hope...
not because of anything I have done, but because You
give my ordinary life eternal value.

I wonder where I will find You during my day. The
more I seek things of You, the more I will notice Your
hand on my life.

Commitment

The Arc of a Promise

I establish my covenant with you: Never again will
all life be cut off by the waters of a flood; never
again will there be a flood to destroy the earth.

GENESIS 9:11

Through the smear of water on my windshield today, I could just make out the road ahead. The wipers cut into my field of vision, and the rhythm of their motion lulled me into deep thoughts. Funny how moments like this bring me to questions about my life. Either I have concern about my day ahead or I have unfounded worries tied to my unknown future. But just as I pulled into a parking lot, I saw a brilliant rainbow framing the landscape beyond my reach. What a glorious reminder that You are committed to my today and to the days that are out of my reach.

As I thank You for the beauty of such colors against a dark sky, may I remember all the times You carried me from the floods of despair to the highlands of mercy.

Knowing Is Believing

Know therefore that the L ORD your God is God; he is the faithful God, keeping his covenant of love to a thousand generations of those who love him and keep his commands.

DEUTERONOMY 7:9

You are God. You are the God of Adam and Eve. Your hands shaped the universe and every particle within its limitless mass. Every generation that has gone before has felt the presence of Your power. I am following in the footsteps of people who have witnessed Your love and care. Their stories remind me of Your commitment to all of Your creation.

When I feel lost in the swirl of the cosmos, I can grab onto the certainty of this commitment. In turn, my daily commitment to You—to keep Your commands—tethers me to the anchor of faith.

Words of Honor

Simply let your "Yes" be "Yes," and your "No," "No";
anything beyond this comes from the evil one.

MATTHEW 5:37

Recently I offered a halfhearted "yes" instead of sticking with my intended response of "no." Other times I will decline the very thing I should be agreeing to. Help me make wise decisions, Lord. If my unwillingness to do something can be traced to laziness or lack of compassion, then lead me into a solid "yes." When a decision could distract me from the priorities You have for me, give my voice strength as I say "no."

I long to clearly discern the Holy Spirit's leading. Make me sensitive to Your calling on my life so that my answers and path can be straight and true.

I Give You This Day

Commit to the LORD whatever you do, and your plans will succeed.

PROVERBS 16:3

Every moment that unfolds today is Yours. I commit my thoughts, my actions, my reactions, and my plans to You. I pray for Your blessing upon my life, and I seek Your strength when I face difficulties that might tempt me to falter from Your way.

When I begin to think "this is just any ol' day," give me a clearer sense of how great this day can be. My offerings, small and large, can be used by You to turn the next 24 hours into a great future.

Hope

Finding Purpose in Hope

May integrity and uprightness protect me, because my hope is in you.

PSALM 25:21

With hope in my heart, I am stronger and lighter. A soul affected by hope is no longer bound to the weight of everyday transgressions. Hope gives wings to my dreams and inspires me to goodness. With your help, I can step up to a task with integrity and honesty. When the daily grind feels redundant, my hope in You helps me clearly see the purpose that is before me.

So much will be born out of hope today. May I recognize the gifts of security and faith and use them to hold me up when nothing else will.

Hope Endures the Wait

We wait in hope for the LORD; he is our help and our shield.

PSALM 33:20

Today I will need help. No doubt about it. I seek You as my source of help and protection. Guide my steps, my words, my inclinations. I also have some burdens to give You. They are worries I have carried around for awhile. But rather than wait for something bad to materialize from these frets, I will wait for Your hope.

Knowing me, I will want to visit my worries from time to time. It is not easy to change my ways. Nevertheless, I trust in You. And I welcome hope into my life now that there is plenty of room.

Holding Fast

Let us hold unswervingly to the hope we profess,
for he who promised is faithful.

HEBREWS 10:23

I can never make up my mind when ordering from a menu. A part of me wants everything listed. The other part of me is scared that as soon as I make my choice, I will realize it was the wrong one. God, don't let me be this way with my profession of hope. Let my belief in Your promises be strong, decisive, and complete.

Life offers many choices. And with each one, there is a risk. But my hope in You, Lord, is never a risk.

A Life of Hope

Be joyful in hope, patient in affliction, faithful in prayer. Share with God's people who are in need. Practice hospitality.

ROMANS 12:12-13

This week, I would love to be a spokesperson for hope. Not in billboard and commercial kinds of ways, but in gentle, subtle ways. Let me translate the hope I receive through faith so others can discern it. Grace me with kind speech and a willing spirit.

When I can step away from my selfish concerns and see the needs of others, I will fully embrace the intention of hope.

Provision

Turning First to You

I sought the LORD, and he answered me; he delivered me from all my fears.

PSALM 34:4

When I seek You during my day, I will be reminded that You are the source of all that I need. Instead of looking to others to make my way easier, I will seek Your wisdom and strength. Instead of relying on my job to build me up, I will seek an identity grounded in You. Each time a need surfaces, let my thoughts go to You, my Creator.

Today I will encounter many opportunities to receive from You. May I be mindful each time Your provision protects me, covers me, and nurtures me.

What Comes from You

*The LORD said to Moses, "I have heard the grum-
bling of the Israelites. Tell them, 'At twilight you
will eat meat, and in the morning you will be filled
with bread. Then you will know that I am the
LORD your God.'-"*

EXODUS 16:11-12

How many times have You met my cries for help
with perfect provision? And how many of those times
have I not even noticed? Lord, give me eyes to see what
comes from Your hand. My grumblings go on for so
long that I have no voice left with which to praise You,
and yet You still extend mercy.

Turn my whining into rejoicing. May every gift I
receive from You be an opportunity to tell others of
Your provision and forgiveness.

A Cause for Goodness

*Our people must learn to devote themselves to
doing what is good, in order that they may provide
for daily necessities and not live unproductive lives.*

TITUS 3:14

I know that before the day is over, I will have
labeled numerous things "good." My morning latté, a
conversation with a friend, a new recipe, a television
show. But what will come from my lips, my hands that
is truly good in Your eyes, Lord? I pray to have a day
filled with goodness that affects people. I pray that my
productivity moves me forward in Your will.

Devotion is not a word used too much these days.
But I hope I can take on a spirit of devotion as I discover ways to bring goodness to light and to honor
goodness when it crosses my path.

May I Have a Miracle?

God gave Solomon wisdom and very great insight,
and a breadth of understanding as measureless as
the sand on the seashore.

1 KINGS 4:29

I don't feel very wise today. Just the act of getting dressed and heading out the door was draining, and now I am supposed to head into my day with purpose. God, expand my spirit, my heart, and my soul so that I can take in every bit of wisdom and understanding You give me. Stretch my sense of knowledge so I will have a heavenly perspective about what truly matters.

On days like this, when it seems a miracle for me to function, I pray for the provision of godly perspective. When I quit trying to be wise and learn to rest in Your ways, I do believe life will open up in extraordinary ways. May this be the day I make that so.

Perseverance

Making It Through

*So do not throw away your confidence; it will
be richly rewarded. You need to persevere so that
when you have done the will of God, you will
receive what he has promised.*

HEBREWS 10:35-36

"If I can just get through this...."

I find myself repeating this statement often. I look
for the silver lining that will make a current task toler-
able. My eyes scan the horizon for the crossroads that
will offer me an alternative to the burden of today.
Perseverance is a requirement of faith. I thank You for
this part of the journey because I believe perseverance
is also a gift.

When I do get through whatever is on my plate
for today, I know I will receive the promises You have
for me. If I do not know the sweat of the work, I will
never know the sweetness of the victory.

Love One Another

Keep on loving each other as brothers.

HEBREWS 13:1

Lord, help me. Today I will encounter a person who usually causes me to stumble. I get defensive in his presence. I'm not even myself when he enters the room. Why do I allow my emotions to get the best of me and turn a situation from good to bad? I am giving this situation over to You. And I am asking to see this person through Your eyes rather than through my tainted lens of past experiences.

I feel good about this. I have never turned my interactions with this person over to the power of prayer. Now I will persevere in Your strength and not my own…and that will change everything.

Gift of Compassion

As you know, we consider blessed those who have
persevered. You have heard of Job's perseverance
and have seen what the Lord finally brought about.
The Lord is full of compassion and mercy.

JAMES 5:11

My mind goes to several friends today, Lord. They all are in need of Your healing touch. Their journeys are filled with great difficulties. The darkness of fear covers their thoughts even as they pray for hope. I pray that their perseverance leads them to blessings You will bring about. In their pain, You offer compassion and comfort. In their worry and uncertainty, You offer mercy.

I want to be a friend who encourages. Give me Your words as I speak to my friends and lift them up in prayer.

Contentment

Open for Joy

Create in me a pure heart, O God, and renew a
steadfast spirit within me....Restore to me the joy
of your salvation and grant me a willing spirit, to
sustain me.

PSALM 51:10,12

Let today be a clean slate that welcomes the hope
and joy ahead, Lord. I no longer want to wake up to
thoughts of many losses, mistakes, or "should've" sce-
narios. As soon as I begin that tally, the day's potential
joy is already lost.

Restore to me the joy of my salvation when I felt
the impact of a clean spirit. I was buoyed by the release
of my burdens to Your care. I not only accepted joy but
watched for it to be a part of my experience. Time and
circumstances have jaded that view. Remind me of the
contentment of faith.

Two Steps Forward...

But godliness with contentment is great gain. For we brought nothing into the world, and we can take nothing out of it. But if we have food and clothing, we will be content with that.

1 TIMOTHY 6:6-8

Why am I so quick to grab things? Stuff consumes me. It fills my home. My thoughts. My space. I don't even want most of these things. Even with a discerning mind in this head of mine, I have given myself over to the marketing monster. I consider this foolish behavior and, beyond that, I consider the acquisition of things as irrelevant to a worthy life. God, remove this lust from my heart so that godly contentment will again be a part of my journey.

Pare away the trivial so that I might truly see what is of Your hands. May I learn to recognize what resources You give me to use in this journey so that I might discover the life You intended for me.

What a Friend

You have made known to me the path of life; you will fill me with joy in your presence, with eternal pleasures at your right hand.

PSALM 16:11

I am excited to think of spending time with a good friend today. We are able to talk about the real stuff of life and also give ourselves over to laughter that is true and deep. We're never self-conscious together. Lord, I know that in Your presence, You offer a friendship as vulnerable and joyful as this earthly one. I'm ashamed to say that I have forgotten this at times and have entered into Your presence like a scolded child rather than a person intending to experience the pleasures of being known and loved and cherished.

You carve out the path of my days through the history of time and experience. Help me step into the joy as well. And may I learn to rush into Your presence with great expectations for contentment and lasting relationship.

Giving It Over

*Submit to God and be at peace with him; in this
way prosperity will come to you.*

JOB 22:21

My restless spirit will not find peace until I come
to You and ask You to take all of my life and shape
it into being. You formed me in my mother's womb,
yet I still hold tightly to what I claim to be "mine,"
including victories and worries. This does not allow
me peace. Give me a glimpse today of what it means
to give myself over to You fully. Walk me through this
important lesson so I will release my grip.

Prosperity, trials, and the storms of life will be man-
ageable and even welcomed when I know they, too,
are under Your submission in my life. No longer will
such changes and circumstances cause my spirit to be
anxious and uncertain.

Now

The Covering of a Life

*If that is how God clothes the grass of the field,
which is here today and tomorrow is thrown into
the fire, will he not much more clothe you, O you
of little faith?*

MATTHEW 6:30

As I get dressed for the day, I know that I am
really facing the day naked and dependant upon You
to clothe me. Your grace clothes me with forgiveness.
Your mercy clothes me with compassion. Your love
covers me with value. I do not make a decision during
my day that does not rely on Your hand.

My faith has been small in many ways, but that was
in the past. I want to outgrow that old faith so that I
can be dressed in the faith You have for me now.

One Thing at a Time

Therefore do not worry about tomorrow, for
tomorrow will worry about itself. Each day has
enough trouble of its own.

MATTHEW 6:34

Slow me down, God. I use my energy each morning troubleshooting for the days ahead. I completely bypass the gift of today, the gift of now. Calm my spirit, expand my breaths, fill me with Your peace so that my spinning thoughts settle. I serve no greater good by thinking ahead, wringing my hands, and wondering what might happen.

Save me from my need to control every situation or possible situation. Lead me back to trusting You with all that will happen. I know that You do not ask me to handle everything on my own. You will be there with me, for me. So today, this moment is only about this moment. May I rest in it and experience it as You intended.

Seeking the Words

Whenever you are arrested and brought to trial, do not worry beforehand about what to say. Just say whatever is given you at the time, for it is not you speaking, but the Holy Spirit.

MARK 13:11

Give me the words I need. I have fretted over today's situation for some time now, and I realize how useless that worrying was. Just as You provide my daily bread, You will provide the words and thoughts I need when pressures exist. Remove the spirit of fear that sweeps over me. Allow me to listen to the Holy Spirit for my leading.

I can rework phrases in my head now and hope everything turns out later. Or I can keep my thoughts on You and know You will take care of me when the time comes.

Following Your Lead

*Love the L*ORD *your God with all your heart and
with all your soul and with all your strength.
These commandments that I give you today are to
be upon your hearts.*

DEUTERONOMY 6:5-6

God, I want to use my many moments today to
love You completely. When I catch myself wandering in
thought, I will begin to praise You. When my day lacks
energy, I will pray for Your love to act through me. Fill
my soul with understandings of You and Your ways so
that my "now" is infused with Your presence.

Carve on my heart all that You hope for my life,
Lord. I will follow this map each step of the way.

Renewal

Finding You

If a man dies, will he live again? All the days of my hard service I will wait for my renewal to come. You will call and I will answer you; you will long for the creature your hands have made.

JOB 14:14-15

Whatever trouble today brings, I know the situation will be restored in Your time. I have great relief knowing that my hard times will be shaped into good things. All I need to do is remember my life before I met You and I understand what a new life is all about. Grace. Second chances. Renewal.

I long for You. The pace of my day might cause me to forget this, but in the quiet moments between sleep and wakefulness I feel the pull toward Your presence. And my joy deepens when I realize You long for me as well.

Shine

*Restore us, O Lord God Almighty; make your face
shine upon us, that we may be saved.*

PSALM 80:19

Some days are just colder than others. I need to
feel the warmth of Your face shining upon me, Lord.
I want to be covered by Your radiance. Resting in the
palm of Your hand, I feel secure and saved. Lead me
back to this place.

Your promises will unfold as the day progresses.
And I will gather these even as I am uncertain about
how the day will play out because through Your promises come renewal and wholeness.

Resurrection's Power

*We were therefore buried with him through
baptism into death in order that, just as Christ
was raised from the dead through the glory of the
Father, we too may live a new life.*

ROMANS 6:4

My personal resurrection seems to be taking place
slowly. I know that You gave me a new life when I gave
my heart to You, but Lord, sometimes I fall back into
the ways of old. I want the renewal given to me by
grace through Your resurrection. I want to see, taste,
and feel what it means to live as a freshly conceived
creation.

You carry me through the pain of death to the glo-
ries of life. Yet some days, like today, I do very little to
follow You wholeheartedly. Your love—it surprises me.
And just when I feel hopeless, You give me a sign of
renewal. An idea. A song. A prayer. A friend. A hope.
This is resurrection in motion in my life.

The Next New Thing

You were taught, with regard to your former way of life, to put off your old self, which is being corrupted by its deceitful desires; to be made new in the attitude of your minds; and to put on the new self, created to be like God in true righteousness and holiness.

EPHESIANS 4:22-24

People talk about new attitudes, new ways of thinking, new ways of being. I tried that in the past, and it was very difficult to maintain whatever new thing I was trying to incorporate into my life. I wanted others to identify me with this new choice, yet I wouldn't try it on long enough for this to happen.

It is only when renewal of the mind and spirit occurs that transformation takes place. My earlier changes were surface level, never intended to be life-changing. Only this choice I make to be Yours will result in a new self worth noticing.

Trials

When Trouble Comes

*If any of you lacks wisdom, he should ask God,
who gives generously to all without finding fault,
and it will be given to him. But when he asks,
he must believe and not doubt, because he who
doubts is like a wave of the sea, blown and tossed
by the wind.*

JAMES 1:5-6

I find myself in a bit of a predicament, as You already know, I'm sure. This morning finds me facing some drama in my life. I have nobody to blame except myself. I denied Your wisdom even though You offered it to me. I turned my back on the leading of the Holy Spirit. This sounds all negative, but in truth, this situation has led me back to You. Every time I forget who really is in control, I end up playing a role in some silly dilemma that could have been avoided.

I would say "never again," but I have said that before. I will just say thank You for giving me the resources to work my way through this trial. And may I turn to You sooner than later next time.

Tuning In to You

I urge you, brothers, by our Lord Jesus Christ and by the love of the Spirit, to join me in my struggle by praying to God for me.

ROMANS 15:30

A tug on my heart this morning leads me to pray for my friends who are going through difficulties. I tuck them in my mind for thought throughout the day, but You know how busy the day becomes. Starting off my day by lifting up others in prayer tunes my heart to be prayerful and mindful of these people all day—even when busy.

Grant me a prayerful nature. It takes work for me to practice this discipline, Lord, yet it also offers me a closeness with You that I long for. I draw near to You right now and pray for myself and others that our trials will lead us back to You always.

Life Work Ahead

*No discipline seems pleasant at the time, but
painful. Later on, however, it produces a harvest of
righteousness and peace for those who have been
trained by it.*

HEBREWS 12:11

How much work is required of me? Some days I
think I am stuck on a treadmill rather than on a road
that leads somewhere. What do You ask of me, God? I
know that most often I am running to follow the commands that come from others, myself, and the world
around me—and not from You.

Help me see that the good work I do will have a
harvest of righteousness. And let me identify the work
I am racing to complete that serves no purpose other
than feeding my ego. Give me the strength to choose
that which serves You.

Spiritual Student

Come to me, all you who are weary and burdened,
and I will give you rest. Take my yoke upon you
and learn from me, for I am gentle and humble in
heart, and you will find rest for your souls. For my
yoke is easy and my burden is light.

MATTHEW 11:28-30

If I can look at my current trial as a form of education, I can almost deal with all that it is costing me—time, energy, heartache, headaches. But this also means that I need to follow the way of my teacher. And You are my teacher for life. All that I need to know and learn comes from my source of life and grace.

Bring me into Your classroom every morning. When I sit at the back of the class, awaken my spirit and call on me, Lord. I am a pupil who needs to see what the Master has for me. You do not give me problems just for the sake of entertainment. You allow these problems so that I will come to You and ask for rest, guidance, and a lesson in faith.

Promise

Trust Takes Trial

*You know with all your heart and soul that not
one of all the good promises the LORD your
God gave you has failed. Every promise has been
fulfilled; not one has failed.*

JOSHUA 23:14

It is easy to forget all that You have brought me
through. Not because I am not grateful but because
after a fall, I am always quick to embrace life and goodness. I don't want to look back or dwell on the troubles
I have experienced. But I am realizing how important it
is to look at these times. They strengthen my journey.

Today, I begin a new kind of trial. I have never been
here before…not exactly. But all I need to do is recall
the promises You have planted in my spirit, and I trust
You once again. The good news—even if the trials are
not getting easier, the trusting is.

Resting in the Unknowing

As you do not know the path of the wind, or how the body is formed in a mother's womb, so you cannot understand the work of God, the Maker of all things.

ECCLESIASTES 11:5

I am clueless how today will turn out. Why do I even bother to guess, assume, or presume anything? I'm so ridiculous that way. Wanting to feign I am in control because times are hard. I cannot know the big picture. I do know You are the one for me to trust. I have examples of Your goodness and faithfulness in my life. I cling to these.

When people ask me what I am going to do or even why something is happening, I no longer want to fabricate my actions or make up reasons. I want to rest in the unknowing. I want to rest in the security of my Maker's plan, come what may.

The Power of a Plan

"For I know the plans I have for you," declares the
LORD, "plans to prosper you and not to harm you,
plans to give you hope and a future."

JEREMIAH 29:11

Is this really the way to go? Personally, I wouldn't have done things this way, but You are God and I am so very human. My vision is limited and failing. I tend to hold on to people or things that really are meant to be released. And I second guess everything. I'm not telling You anything You don't already know.

But do You know that today I woke up and felt excited about the plan You have for me? I have finally given myself over to the idea of the future being about hope and not fear. It's a new thing for me, but I think I could get used to it.

Awareness

Learning to Be Aware

Know also that wisdom is sweet to your soul; if
you find it, there is a future hope for you, and
your hope will not be cut off.

PROVERBS 24:14

Recently I have moved through my days in a bit of
a fog. I look back on the past week, month even, and
sense that I have not been aware of You and the lessons
You would have me learn. I don't want to be someone
who mentally checks out of life. Even when I face difficulties, I will glean wisdom that feeds my soul.

Make me aware of what You would have me learn
today, Lord.

In the Wake of a Day

Hear, O Israel, and be careful to obey so that it
may go well with you and that you may increase
greatly in a land flowing with milk and honey, just
as the LORD, the God of your fathers, promised you.

DEUTERONOMY 6:3

This morning I turned off my alarm, sat on the
edge of the bed, and just listened to You. Before the
flood of plans, thoughts, regrets, or schedule changes
filled the space between my ears, I used my ears to take
in Your directions.

I pray to be aware of what You ask of me so that I
can obey faithfully. I want to walk in Your ways so that
I can step into Your promises.

Me Me Me

*Hear and pay attention, do not be arrogant, for
the LORD has spoken.*

JEREMIAH 13:15

I never thought my pride could actually block me
from understanding You. But these days, I am stubborn—always trying to figure out the way on my own.
I speak up on behalf of myself, my opinions, and my
ego more often than I speak up for my faith. I let my
concerns consume me before I turn to You in prayer.

So much me and so little You makes for a difficult
life. I miss Your gentle leading. My mind and heart are
too scattered to take in Your truths. I don't even taste
the simple joys because I deem them insignificant.
Help me strip away my own agenda and prideful ways
so that I have nothing blocking my view of You.

Taking Notice

Then he returned to his disciples and found them sleeping. "Could you men not keep watch with me for one hour?" he asked Peter. "Watch and pray so that you will not fall into temptation. The spirit is willing, but the body is weak."

MATTHEW 26:40-41

Will You catch me sleeping today instead of being alert? How many chances do I miss to do right, to do good, or to serve another? Please open my eyes to those I meet who need help that I can offer. Sharpen my mind so I can be discerning.

When I am tired, it is easy for me to fall back into old, bad habits. Grant me the energy to be careful and wise. When the wisdom I need is beyond my capacity, give me Your wisdom to see the way through a situation.

Courage

Carry Me

Let the morning bring me word of your unfailing
love, for I have put my trust in you. Show me the
way I should go, for to you I lift up my soul.

PSALM 143:8

I feel like such a child. Today gives me too much worry and grief and stress. I thought I could do it—carry out the day—but I cannot. I need You, God. I not only need You to be with me, but I need You to carry me through this day of mine. I started out so strong, but now that I face the reality of moving forward, I cannot go it alone.

Show me the way. I lift up my day to You and pray for courage to keep going. I trust You. And where there is still resistance to rely on You instead of myself, please remind me of this feeling in the pit of my stomach. You are my only source of strength.

Needing a Savior

Those who know your name will trust in you, for
you, LORD, have never forsaken those who seek you.

PSALM 9:10

I come to Your presence today with a bit of a
sheepish look and a heavy heart. I have been here
before—countless times—and You have not forsaken
me. But I feel so needy that sometimes I second-guess
returning to You. But I know Your name, and You are
my Holy Redeemer. You are my Savior and Messiah. It
is grace that falls from Your lips, not a gavel of convic-
tion when I am humble and in need.

God, grant me the peace that comes with Your
strength and courage. Do not let me turn my back on
You when I so desperately require Your guidance.

Returning to the Boat

Immediately he spoke to them and said, "Take courage! It is I. Don't be afraid." Then he climbed into the boat with them, and the wind died down. They were completely amazed.

MARK 6:50-51

Do I even recognize You when You enter my boat to calm the storms and save my soul? Have I ever looked past You as I watch for a Savior who seems bigger, stronger, and more able to pull me from the clutches of the waves? I know I have because my self-doubt can make my faith weak. Yet You are faithful each time, and my worries fade.

I do take courage in You. I will not look beyond Your shoulders to the night sky in search of more. I will trust You. You are the One who returns to the boat of my life and tells me not to be afraid.

Thirst

The Hunger of the Void

Blessed are those who hunger and thirst for righteousness, for they will be filled.

MATTHEW 5:6

Sometimes I skate over the voids in my life. I don't even look down to see if the chasm still exists because I don't want to know. But days like today I cannot get up without asking for You to fill that void. I know it is there, and I know I cannot skate, skip, or jump over it—even in a state of denial. The hunger comes from deep within and it does not fade when I puff up my own ego or worth.

My hunger and thirst leads me back to Your righteousness, Lord. Only You can fill this place that questions, that missteps, that becomes empty when ignored. Fill this place in me and let it overflow to all that I do and am.

Seeing the Answer

He humbled you, causing you to hunger and then feeding you with manna, which neither you nor your fathers had known, to teach you that man does not live on bread alone but on every word that comes from the mouth of the LORD.

DEUTERONOMY 8:3

When I ask You for wealth, what do You send instead? When I ask for bread, what nourishment do You bestow upon me and my family? When I lack, what do You give to me to make up for my weakness? All that carries me into my life and through it comes from Your hand and Your way of sustenance.

When my stomach growls, I may question what I see fall from heaven to fill my plate. But, Lord, I receive these gifts with faith and with the belief that You are guiding my journey—and You do not leave Your children to starve.

Beyond Reasons

For I was hungry and you gave me something to
eat, I was thirsty and you gave me something to
drink, I was a stranger and you invited me in, I
needed clothes and you clothed me, I was sick and
you looked after me, I was in prison and you came
to visit me.

MATTHEW 25:35-36

The needs of my brothers and sisters around me
are so great, I do not know where to start. There is a
strong desire, a thirst to quench, to reach out and help
others. But then I sit back and list the stipulations or
the reasons this could go very wrong. This is when I
think of You asking us to feed, clothe, and aid the sick,
and visit the imprisoned, and it is clear You do not ask
me to ask, You ask me to serve.

May I truly see You in those I will help today. And
when I cannot, give me the strength to continue giving.
Because even when I am blind to You, You are the one
who stands before me asking for more.

Learning to Knock

*Ask and it will be given to you; seek and you will
find; knock and the door will be opened to you. For
everyone who asks receives; he who seeks finds;
and to him who knocks, the door will be opened.*

MATTHEW 7:7-8

Maybe I have lived through too many fund-raisers
as a kid to feel comfortable enough to stand in front
of a door and knock. I think about the possible rejec-
tion and ignore the desire in me to know the One on
the other side. I consider other ways I could go about
asking for assistance—the phone, a letter, an e-mail...a
prayer—and they seem so much better suited to my
personality.

Lord, get my clenched fingers to start knocking.
The excuses rush over my good intentions like a tidal
wave. Yet I understand that first You require us to come
to You...humbled, seeking, and thirsty. This is when
You answer the door. But first, I must knock.

Responsibility

Living the Work

All hard work brings a profit, but mere talk leads only to poverty.

PROVERBS 14:23

I hit the snooze button on the alarm several times this morning. I started to pray and then ended up venting about the work I have to get done today. Now I'm back and thanking You for the work I have to do because I know it is a gift from You. My venting leads to nothing productive or fruitful. It only builds the toxic thoughts in my mind and heart.

But hard work has its own reward of faithfulness, results, labor, and sacrifice. It is also a chance for me to sense the thrill of creation—even if in a very minor way. Lord, take the work that is before me and shape it into a worthwhile effort. I have rolled up my sleeves, and I am now ready to receive this beneficial part of life.

Stay

Brothers, each man, as responsible to God, should remain in the situation God called him to.

1 CORINTHIANS 7:24

Surely You jest. This is what I am thinking sometimes as I head into the situation You have placed me in lately. This couldn't possibly be of God...of Your hand. Could it? Lord, give me perspective on this. Maybe I just want to avoid this kind of responsibility. It seems there is rarely a break from it. Maybe there are other lessons You want me to learn right now.

I will remain here because You remain beside me. I cannot do this alone. Please help me see inklings of the purpose of this time and place in my life. If not now, sometime soon. When I do not see the reason, please give me the inspiration.

Motivated by Love

*And now, dear lady, I am not writing you a new
command but one we have had from the
beginning. I ask that we love one another.
And this is love: that we walk in obedience to his
commands. As you have heard from the beginning,
his command is that you walk in love.*

2 JOHN 5-6

From the beginning of the day until the passing of
the night beneath the stars, I pray that I follow the command that is born of Your will—to love one another.
Give me Your heart for others so that my thoughts
turn to compassion and unity rather than judgment
and separation.

I pray for this day and all those to come…each one
an opportunity to show You to the world and to show
You my faithfulness. It is out of gratitude that I step
into my morning. It is with humility that I turn to You
throughout the day. Lead me with love so that I may
follow in the path of love forever.

One-
Minute
Prayers™

to End
Your Day

High Above

He also made the stars. God set them in the
expanse of the sky to give light on the earth, to
govern the day and the night, and to separate light
from darkness. And God saw that it was good.

GENESIS 1:16-18

Stars twinkle beyond my reach, but not above my faith. Nothing exceeds the extent of my hope in You. When I consider the people of the world, there are too many to count. Am I not just one of Your many children? How do You have time to hear my prayers, my concerns, my celebrations?

Then I consider how You made the stars. You placed them with care in the sky. There are so many—too many to count. Yet Your care is evident when those night beacons shine brightly and lead me back to belief in a God who knows me intimately, personally, and who hears each prayer that leaves my lips.

Transformation

First Time

And God said, "Let there be light," and there was
light. God saw that the light was good, and he
separated the light from the darkness. God called
the light "day," and the darkness he called "night."
And there was evening, and there was morning—
the first day.

GENESIS 1:3-5

I wonder what the first night looked like. How did
You arrange the sky? Did You watch the sun go down
and imagine how Your future creation would love the
sight of such beauty?

Lord, I thank You for that time when day becomes
night. I allow that time to come and go so very often
without speaking words of gratitude. Tonight I paid
attention to how You transformed the view from my
window. It reminded me of the hope I have in how You
are transforming me.

Goodness of a Bad Day

*Though outwardly we are wasting away, yet inwardly
we are being renewed day by day. For our light and
momentary troubles are achieving for us an eternal
glory that far outweighs them all.*

2 CORINTHIANS 4:16-17

Today was a series of errors, miscommunications,
and missteps. It'd be nice to forget about the day, but I
know that while I am experiencing those bumps in the
road there are more eternal activities in play.

When I stumble, there is still victory. You transform
my very human errors into pearls of internal value. I
have learned humility, perseverance, faith, and patience.
Not bad for a day's work.

New Thoughts

Do not conform any longer to the pattern of this world, but be transformed by the renewing of your mind.

ROMANS 12:2

I like stability. I like it so much that I unintentionally create each day to look the same as the last. I fall into ruts that do nothing to serve You or this life You have given to me. I pray for the wisdom to infuse my life with renewal and possibility.

When I am burdened with repetition and routine, remind me how much each day is worth. Change my thinking when I maneuver on autopilot. I don't want to waste the chance to think differently, feel differently, and to taste the different moments that add up to my lifetime.

Flip of a Switch

I will turn the darkness into light before them and
make the rough places smooth.

ISAIAH 42:16

Just like that, day is night. And when I am sleeping, the switch is flipped the other direction and night becomes day. God, You orchestrate the universe without need of my help. Your power does not depend on me. I am so humbled that You work through me, and that You see value in who I am and in this life I am living.

I find peace tonight, resting in the knowledge that You orchestrated my existence. You turn my personal night—the rough places I stumble over—into smooth paths that reflect Your light. I am in good hands...they are shaping me into a better person, just like that.

Awareness

Ritual

Every morning and evening they present burnt offerings and fragrant incense to the LORD.

2 CHRONICLES 13:11

I gave You my day today, Lord. With great intention, I handed over my emotions, my worries, my work, my relationships, and my steps. I feel the difference as the day comes to a close. I am more aware of how You are a part of all that I am, do, say, and feel. Oh, how many days I have wasted by not being aware of this truth!

Help me give my day to You again tomorrow. May I start and end all my days by presenting to You the offering of my life, of myself. And may this sacrifice be pleasing to You.

Forecast

[Jesus] replied, "When evening comes, you say, 'It will be fair weather, for the sky is red,' and in the morning, 'Today it will be stormy, for the sky is red and overcast.' You know how to interpret the appearance of the sky, but you cannot interpret the signs of the times."

MATTHEW 16:2-3

I love to check the weather forecasts for the week. When I gather all the facts I feel more in control. I receive a sense of security. Getting the temperatures, examining the details, and knowing how the clouds will cover the sky might help me plan a family picnic, but that does not give me Your full knowledge or Your power.

I don't have to know what the weather is for tomorrow. Life is not built on predictions. It is built on Your truth, rain or shine.

Loose Change

Command them to do good, to be rich in good deeds, and to be generous and willing to share. In this way they will lay up treasure for themselves as a firm foundation for the coming age, so that they may take hold of the life that is truly life.

1 TIMOTHY 6:18-19

When I come home, I reach into my pockets and remove any coins remaining from a day of spending. A jar on the counter holds these leftover portions that I once considered hardly worth saving. As the jar grows heavy, I understand the power of accumulation.

Lord, help me be aware of ways to spend goodness throughout the day. May I never consider a portion of kindness too small or insignificant to receive or give. I know that each act of compassion accumulates in heaven.

Counting Before Sleep

How precious to me are your thoughts, O God!
How vast is the sum of them! Were I to count
them, they would outnumber the grains of sand.
When I awake, I am still with you.

PSALM 139:17-18

After a day of multitasking and problem solving, I
have a hard time unwinding. My thoughts can rev up,
spiral down, or pull me toward energy when I would
rather be resting. I turn to You and seek Your thoughts,
God. Fill my mind and my heart with Your peaceful,
living words. When I call out to You, You are there.

Ending my day with You, Lord, gives me the security I have always longed for. I know that when I am
awake, You will be with me. And when I am asleep,
You are with me then too.

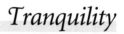

Tranquility

As the Storm Passes

*[Jesus] got up and rebuked the wind and the
raging waters; the storm subsided, and all was
calm. "Where is your faith?" he asked his disciples.*

LUKE 8:24-25

When the air stirs about me, when the wind blows
from all directions, when I cannot stand because of the
pressure around me...I want to be a person of faith.
My eyes peer toward the dark night, and I cannot dis-
tinguish shapes. There is so much left unknown. Yet
my heart does not race and my mind does not doubt
because I know where my faith is—it is in the hope
of the moment, it is in the belief that the storm will
pass, it is in the assurance that Your peace overcomes
everything I will face.

Who I Am

Finally, all of you, live in harmony with one another; be sympathetic, love as brothers, be compassionate and humble.

1 PETER 3:8

My mind mellows now, and I sit back, glad to be done with a busy day. Evening's tranquility presents a chance to settle in with myself and with You. It is the time of day that I most often reflect on who I am and what my life means.

I am filled with the desire to be more like You in every way. I want to feel compassion for others. I want to love my neighbor as myself. I want sympathy to turn my heart toward empathy. I want to follow Your ways and always know who I am—Your child.

My Haven

*He stilled the storm to a whisper; the waves of the
sea were hushed. They were glad when it grew
calm, and he guided them to their desired haven.*

PSALM 107:29-30

I am glad to put my feet up. My bones were weary
today. I felt frazzled when I had to juggle two things
at once. My mouth barely functioned when I had to
speak. Oh, how I longed for this moment to breathe
deeply without the pressure to perform or please.

Lord, the whirlwind of worldly demands sometimes consumes me. Turn my thoughts to You and my
heart toward the peace You offer. When I do, I know
You will lead me to the haven of Your shelter.

What I Hold Tonight

They will speak of the glorious splendor of your majesty, and I will meditate on your wonderful works.

PSALM 145:5

How lucky I am to see evidence of Your love and beauty. It surrounds me. Every moment offers a glimpse of Your caring touch if I open my eyes to it. Nature attests to Your splendor. A community gathering together during a time of need shines with Your brilliance. A child's unfiltered joy reflects Your own.

Lord, I cradle these images of You in my soul tonight. I meditate on Your wonderful works because they speak of Your goodness and faithfulness.

Darkness

When Darkness Follows

*But let him remember the days of darkness, for
they will be many.*

ECCLESIASTES 11:8

As night falls, it feels very familiar. My heart knows
it well even during the daylight hours. A heaviness, the
blanket of worry, covers me lately. Lord, bring me out
of this constant night. Allow me to remember the days
of darkness from before because when I think of them,
I also am reminded of Your saving grace.

Walk with me through this time of shadows. Keep
the darkness from following me into tomorrow. Protect
me with the covering of hope.

Not Me, Lord

When evening came, Jesus was reclining at the
table with the Twelve. And while they were eating,
he said, "I tell you the truth, one of you will betray
me." They were very sad and began to say to him
one after the other, "Surely not I, Lord?"

MATTHEW 26:20-22

Under the cloak of darkness, it is easy to lie. It
is easy to even tell myself half-truths when I am certain that I can stay protected by the veil of shadows.
Thoughts that would seem impossible during the cheer
of day, now flood my mind and weigh me down.

Lord, turn my negativity into an opportunity for
healing. In the past I have said, "Surely not I, Lord..."
But now I know how vulnerable I am. I will tell myself
and You the truth: I cannot overcome my self-decep-
tion with self-talk. I need You and Your light to be
present.

My Worth

*For I am poor and needy, and my heart is
wounded within me. I fade away like an evening
shadow; I am shaken off like a locust.*

PSALM 109:22-23

I have been comparing myself to others again. Yes,
this is a road I have taken many times. Why can't I
learn to place my value solely in You rather than in the
fickle preferences of the world? I don't earn enough,
have enough, know enough…I am not enough when
I stand alone.

Only You can shine light upon my beauty. My
goodness exists because I have placed my faith in who
You are. I will never be perfect by comparison to an
ever-changing list of worldly requirements. But I will
always be wealthy, I will have abundance, and I will be
enough when I rest in Your purpose for my life.

The Light Show

You are my lamp, O LORD; the LORD turns my
darkness into light.

2 SAMUEL 22:29

A friend reminded me of how far I had come.
They knew me back when I had sorrow and empti-
ness. Now they notice the light that burns from within.
They remember me when I was eager to turn a good
moment into a gripe session and when I felt encouraged by another's discouragement.

You have turned the direction of my heart, my feet,
my mind, and my actions. Since I have known You,
the frown of yesterday rarely crosses my countenance.
Even when trials are on the horizon, I know to follow
the light of Your way. And You take me far.

Restless

Resting in Promises

Moses also said, "You will know that it was the
LORD when he gives you meat to eat in the evening
and all the bread you want in the morning, because
he has heard your grumbling against him."

EXODUS 16:8

Why don't I learn to be quiet? I have been grumbling about my circumstances for so long that even I cannot bear to listen. When others face bigger troubles, I am quick to suggest my turmoil is of great weight and concern. I tell my story of woe over and over.

Lord, You silence my restless spirit and my rampant complaints. I look around me at the provision so obviously from Your hand, and I am unable to find the silly words that flowed easily before. Peace overcomes me, and I rest in the promises that shine forth even when I do not deserve them.

Which Way to Go?

*Sow your seed in the morning, and at evening let
not your hands be idle, for you do not know which
will succeed, whether this or that, or whether both
will do equally well.*

ECCLESIASTES 11:6

Should I go this way…or that way? Tomorrow I will
face a fork in the road, and both directions will look so
very tempting. This question keeps me awake because
I have allowed myself to become restless. Pacing in the
living room does not still my mind or my heart. Give
me an answer, Lord. Please.

You remind me to fall to my knees in prayer and
supplication and thanksgiving. My hands reach for Your
Word, and this purpose calms them. Now I am feeding
my spirit with certainty over uncertainty. And this night
I give my doubts over to Your control.

Chasing Fears

*So do not worry, saying, "What shall we eat?" or
"What shall we drink?" or "What shall we wear?"
For the pagans run after all these things, and your
heavenly Father knows that you need them. But
seek first his kingdom and his righteousness, and
all these things will be given to you as well.*

MATTHEW 6:31-33

It is futile to chase after fear, for fear leaves in
its wake a very new path of problems. The people I
want to guarantee me security are only people. Their
promises do not mean anything to me and my eternal
future.

I will not waste my time, my day, my evening in
this pursuit of unnecessary concerns. I need not glance
around nervously, anticipating the next problem. You
assure me that I need only to look to You and Your
kingdom. Here true needs are recognized, and they are
filled, satisfied by Your grace.

This, I'm Not Good At

Be still before the Lord and wait patiently for him.

PSALM 37:7

I have loved You for so long, Lord. I have become a person who prays earnestly and with vulnerability. My speech is becoming filled with words of encouragement and hope. I seek Your Word with deep hunger because there were too many years when I sought nourishment from empty sources.

But God...I am not good at being still before You. There is a part of me that wants to rush the process, wants to leap forward to the promise fulfilled, and wants to take the reins of my life from Your hands. Help me grow in patience. Keep me from the desire to disrupt Your plan for my life. I am ready for this lesson.

Refuge

What I Call Sacred

One man considers one day more sacred than
another; another man considers every day alike.
Each one should be fully convinced in his own mind.

ROMANS 14:5

   This time of the evening feels sacred. I believe it
is the point in my day when I am able to give myself
over to Your presence. I want to take this sense of
peace with me into my chaotic days. What a gift that
would be.

   For now I will rest in what I know to be true. You
are here with me. This time of refuge and connection
provides me with a view of Your faithfulness, compassion, and desire to be present with Your child.

Shelter Me

Keep me safe, O God, for in you I take refuge.

PSALM 16:1

Shelter me tonight, Lord. Take me in Your embrace and keep me safe from my past and my future worries. If left on my own, I would not make it through the night without a stream of tears. But here in Your arms I can relax. I think more clearly from this place of refuge.

I used to be a child who didn't know to come in out of the rain. Now I am Your child who knows to come in to Your presence and out of the pain. Don't let go of me, Lord.

Mine and Yours

In your unfailing love you will lead
the people you have redeemed.
In your strength you will guide them
to your holy dwelling.

EXODUS 15:13

This is quite a journey I am on. Each day offers more steps toward Your holy dwelling, Your resting place. When I stumble, You whisper to me that I am worth leading. You reach for my hand and help me to stand and continue.

My weakness is Your strength. My failing is Your victory. My worst-case scenario is Your moment of shining glory. Lord, You shape all my humanness with Your power and grace, and it becomes something new. This is the miraculous journey of redemption.

Refuge Within

Create in me a pure heart, O God, and renew a
steadfast spirit within me.

PSALM 51:10

I have sought to create a sense of refuge in many different ways. I got organized—and that lasted a couple
weeks. I tried some breathing practices to relieve stress
but was afraid I was doing them wrong. I sprinkled
potpourri in my bedroom, but started sneezing.

God, now I understand that my true chance for
refuge will not happen by altering the external factors.
May Your purity stir within me and create a sanctuary
where Your love will make its home.

Solitude

Home with the Lord

We live by faith, not by sight. We are confident, I say, and would prefer to be away from the body and at home with the Lord.

2 CORINTHIANS 5:7-8

As soon as I step away from the conversations with others, the distractions, and the busyness, my heart's first impulse is to run to You. When I am alone and experiencing solitude, I am also experiencing Your presence with more intensity.

During times of aloneness, my faith in You seems clearer, brighter, and stronger. It is because I am leaning on You completely. There is no greater peace than to be at home with You. I have faith that this is a mere echo of what it feels like to go home to heaven.

Head for the Hills

After he had dismissed them, [Jesus] went up on a mountainside by himself to pray. When evening came, he was there alone.

MATTHEW 14:23

I am following Your lead, Lord. I get it now more than ever. Your most difficult times were covered and followed with prayer. After long days of praying over others and healing them, You still yearned to pray to Your Father.

There is so much going on in my life. Good things. Hard things. Some things that I have yet to figure out. I am learning to bring all to You in prayer and to seek Your face no matter the circumstances. It is time to unwind, but my heart is heading for the hills to spend moments of solitude with its Maker.

Hear My Cries

Evening, morning and noon I cry out in distress,
and he hears my voice.

PSALM 55:17

I am like an infant who needs comfort, food, and reassurance around the clock. I cry out to You in the morning when I am pondering what questions the day might present. I seek to connect with You when the day is going full speed and I need a right perspective to survive. In the evening, my cries are even greater. It is the hour of solitude; I need to know that You are with me even as distractions fall away and I am left vulnerable and silent. Hear my cries, Abba Father.

Only You

My soul finds rest in God alone; my salvation comes from him.

PSALM 62:1

Lord, when You look at my past, does it hurt You to see the many times I tried to save myself? Or when I asked others to save me? I avoided being alone with You because I wasn't ready to exchange my version of salvation for Yours. I didn't believe I was worth the grace.

Solitude no longer scares me. I welcome it because my soul rests in Your hands. I don't want to find this comfort anywhere else. Only You can save me. Only now can I see that Your love makes me worthy.

Covering

Completely Covered

But just as you excel in everything—in faith, in speech, in knowledge, in complete earnestness and in your love for us—see that you also excel in this grace of giving.

2 CORINTHIANS 8:7

Did I honor You today, Lord? All day I was striving to be godly when I spoke, made choices, did work, expressed kindness, prayed—I think that covers it. Are You proud of me for making a conscious effort to walk in Your ways?

Now when I am here with You, recapping the day and trying to get a report card summary out of You, I realize how ineffective and faithless this thinking is. You have not called me to be perfect; You have called me to be covered by Your perfect grace.

Gladness

Let all who take refuge in you be glad; let them
ever sing for joy. Spread your protection over them,
that those who love your name may rejoice in you.

PSALM 5:11

I have many blessings, yet my spirit leans toward sorrow or frustration so naturally. Guide me to the refuge of Your mercy, Lord. When I know I am covered by You and cared for by You, I embrace gladness.

My spirits are lifted when I am in fellowship with You. Calling out Your name and relying on Your name brings me deep joy. May I always trust in Your love and comfort, and may I always step under Your protection.

Special Delivery

You are my hiding place; you will protect me from
trouble and surround me with songs of deliverance.

PSALM 32:7

I have my dry cleaning delivered to my home. I can order pizza to arrive at my door within 20 minutes. But there is nothing I can do to deliver myself from the trouble that plagues me tonight. I have tried. I have prayed for You to give me the strength to do it on my own, when all along I needed the protection of Your strength.

It's not easy for me to ask for comfort and help. I am stubborn and human and often conflicted with a false sense of control. Pare away these excuses, Lord. I am in great need, and only You can deliver me.

Banner of Love

See how I love your precepts; preserve my life, O
LORD, according to your love.

PSALM 119:159

I remember singing a song as a child at camp about the banner of Your love. I never understood that song. But now that evening doesn't end with festivities involving marshmallows and bonfires, the meaning of those words is becoming as clear as a summer night's sky.

Beneath the banner of Your love and Your wisdom, my life is preserved. My adult problems outweigh those I took with me to camp, but even so, they are not too great for Your healing and Your grace to cover. This is something to sing about!

Reflection

What Comes to Mind

You kept my eyes from closing; I was too troubled
to speak. I thought about the former days, the years
of long ago; I remembered my songs in the night.

PSALM 77:4-6

I have been staring at the ceiling for hours. I feel
the urgency to talk to You tonight. But there is silence,
so I stare and wonder and ponder. Then I begin to
remember all the times You have been there for me. All
the times I watched with amazement as You shaped a
trial into a treasure.

You speak to me tonight through these remem-
brances. I am not alone. I never have been. And this
is what You remind me of over and over through Your
acts of faithfulness.

Tell Me

*But make up your mind not to worry beforehand
how you will defend yourselves. For I will give you
words and wisdom that none of your adversaries
will be able to resist or contradict.*

LUKE 21:14-15

Just when I think I have everything all figured out,
somebody challenges me or tears down my securities.
The right words never seem to rise to my mind and to
my mouth to dispute what they are saying, so here I
am wanting to figure it all out beforehand. I don't want
any surprises tomorrow. Help me, Lord.

Peace comes over me as I ask for Your help. You
are not going to provide me with advance comments
to memorize before confrontation. Instead, You tell me
to reflect on Your faithfulness and goodness, and the
words and strength I need will be there.

Life Management

The hardworking farmer should be the first to receive
a share of the crops. Reflect on what I am saying, for
the Lord will give you insight into all this.

2 TIMOTHY 2:6-7

I have an entire shelf of life-management books.
They offer some wisdom and some advice, but they
fall short of insight that relates to my life specifically.
How grateful I am that I have Your truth and Your
Word to reflect on.

You don't generalize or tell me the top five ways I
will improve my existence or my bank account. You
tell me there is just one way to manage my life—to
give it over to You. My hard work will possibly reap
character development, financial support, and positive
results. But I never have to earn Your grace—this is the
key to success.

Everything in Its Place

*When I consider your heavens, the work of your
fingers, the moon and the stars, which you have
set in place, what is man that you are mindful of
him, the son of man that you care for him?*

PSALM 8:3-4

Tonight's sky tells me much of Your nature. When I
reflect on the miracle of starlight, the pull of the moon,
the orbit of the earth, and the mysteries of space, I feel
small and insignificant. But then I consider how much
order and brilliance it took to construct this night sky,
and I know what I need to know to have hope: The
same care and attention went into the creation of me.

When You placed my heart just so and aligned
my purpose with Your will, there was nothing left to
chance. I don't need to question whether You think of
me because Your fingers shaped me. This life You have
set in motion is here for a reason.

Dusk

Looking for Light

He has blocked my way so I cannot pass; he has
shrouded my paths in darkness.

JOB 19:8

Dusk covers the road ahead. Different colors are
cast against the sky as though a new artist were on
shift. I squint, trying to see what usually is clear on
the horizon.

I know it is time to get home because soon there
will be no light to ease my journey. My soul craves
more light. You have shrouded my path in darkness.
I cannot continue with my own vision, but must trust
Your sight to lead me through to tomorrow's dawn.

First, Praise

Give glory to the LORD your God before he brings the darkness, before your feet stumble on the darkening hills.

JEREMIAH 13:16

Thank You for today, Lord! I praise Your name and give You the glory for all that was accomplished. May You look at what this servant has done and call it good and right. Today was not easy, but I kept hold of Your Word and my path was secured.

I know the darkness will come. There will be a time when I have trials that pull me from the path and cast me onto the rocky terrain of uncertainty and risk. On this slope I will hold on to my faith—a faith that has been strengthened through my days of praise.

Sins of Shadows

The eye of the adulterer watches for dusk; he thinks, "No eye will see me," and he keeps his face concealed.

JOB 24:15

There are those who seek anonymity as shadows create hiding places ideal for concealing sins—from human eyes. May I never allow the appearance of clouds during times of trial to become my excuse to betray You, Lord.

In faith, there is never an absence of light. Total darkness will not conceal my wrongdoings. Reveal to me any part of my life that has been left to the shadows. Give me the courage to bring indiscretions to You with a spirit of repentance and sorrow so that I never boast with pride that I have kept something from You.

Bright with Belief

But when he asks, he must believe and not doubt,
because he who doubts is like a wave of the sea,
blown and tossed by the wind.

JAMES 1:6

Illuminate the answers, Lord. Convict my spirit and turn me in the direction of clarity and truth. I have doubted in the past, and it made for a very bumpy voyage. When I stare out at the horizon, I want to believe there is a way through the storm. Doubt is a clouding of the mind and heart, and it disturbs any chance I have to navigate with faith.

When I ask for direction and Your beacon shines to guide me, may I never look back to the dark waves behind me. Anchor my belief in the sureness of the shore that is Your purpose and hope.

Worry

Worst Case Scenario

In the morning you will say, "If only it were evening!"
and in the evening, "If only it were morning!"

DEUTERONOMY 28:67

The flip-flop of worry turns my thoughts, my stomach, and my hope upside down. Instead of standing firm in Your promises, I waver back and forth, uncertain of what I want or need. All day I longed for the quiet and solitary nature of night. Now, in the later hours, I can pray fervently to make it until the light of dawn.

Lord, speak to my soul. Grant me the wisdom and faith to see that there is no place or time or situation that will distance me from Your sight or Your peace.

Missing Out

*As evening approached, the disciples came to him
and said, "This is a remote place, and it's already
getting late. Send the crowds away, so they can go
to the villages and buy themselves some food."*

MATTHEW 14:15

I planned and replanned my day today. Yet there
were surprises at every turn. Some were blessings,
some I hope were blessings in disguise…but they all
disrupted my big plans. I like to be efficient, Lord.
When things closed in on me, I became anxious about
the outcome.

But just as You showed the disciples time after time,
there is no need to worry. Things are in Your control.
When I worry, I lose sight of the purpose in that very
moment. Help me see Your hand in everything that
happens—including the detours.

Choke Hold

The one who received the seed that fell among the thorns is the man who hears the word, but the worries of this life and the deceitfulness of wealth choke it, making it unfruitful.

MATTHEW 13:22

I want a faith that flourishes, Lord. I want to hear Your promises and take hold of them and believe in them. But when my worries about money, relationships, or the day's agenda kick in, my faith suffers. My fears stunt its growth, and I am left feeling empty.

Let me be encouraged by other believers and uplifted by creation's wonder. Hope creates a fertile ground where faith can take root and blossom. Guide me toward those people and practices that will inspire me to live a fruitful, abundant life.

Out and In

[The Lord] will never let the righteous fall.

PSALM 55:22

I hung up the phone after talking to a friend about a problem. I sat in my favorite chair with my favorite blanket and dissected the problem further. I made a list of possible solutions but nothing seemed remarkable enough to work, so I kept on worrying. Finally I sought Your Word, Lord, and was reminded to cast my cares on You.

I wanted someone to take my problem away. But Your promise is to walk with me, to sustain me, to hold me up as I make my way through this in Your strength. You pull me out of the despair and promise to never let me fall.

Lessons

Before the Rain

Do the skies themselves send down showers? No, it is you, O LORD our God. Therefore our hope is in you, for you are the one who does all this.

JEREMIAH 14:22

I opened my window tonight during a passing storm. My lungs took in the fresh air, and I was so thankful that the clouds had brought renewal to a thirsty Earth. But before I heard the first drops on my roof, You had commanded the showers. You are behind everything beautiful and wondrous.

Tonight I benefit from Your sweet rain. I learn a lesson about hope: It is to be placed in You, the maker of the smallest and the largest blessings.

In Your Hands

I form the light and create darkness,
I bring prosperity and create disaster;
I, the LORD, do all these things.

ISAIAH 45:7

It is so easy to take credit for accomplishments or milestones in my life. Yet it is You who formed the light and created darkness. This morning I found myself accepting praise for something that was entirely Your doing.

My heart lesson tonight is to give You glory for all that happens. You, Lord, do all that is good in my life and throughout my days. I cheat myself out of a deeper faith when I take credit for wonders shaped by my Creator.

Seed of Faith

I would like to learn just one thing from you: Did you receive the Spirit by observing the law, or by believing what you heard?

GALATIANS 3:2

Does my faith reveal a strong sense of Your saving grace and Your love? I ask tonight because lately my motives seem so much about bringing justice to situations and relationships. I first came to You because of Your compassion and Your forgiveness, so why do I seem determined to pass judgment rather than to give mercy?

Help me learn to treat others with the love You have shown me. Maybe I will plant the seed of faith in another's heart.

Always My Teacher

*When [Jesus] had finished washing their feet, he
put on his clothes and returned to his place. "Do
you understand what I have done for you?" he
asked them. "You call me 'Teacher' and 'Lord,'
and rightly so, for that is what I am. Now that I,
your Lord and Teacher, have washed your feet, you
also should wash one another's feet. I have set you an
example that you should do as I have done for you.*

JOHN 13:12-15

The role models of faith around me are people
who keep learning from You. Give me a hunger for
the lessons You have to teach me. I want to follow
Your example with passion and purpose. When You
washed the feet of Your disciples, You did not call them
to praise You, but to turn around and wash the feet of
others. This is Your powerful lesson to Your children.
May I become a forever student of the Master.

Peace

Daily Sweetness

Light is sweet, and it pleases the eyes to see the sun. However many years a man may live, let him enjoy them all.

ECCLESIASTES 11:7-8

Thank You for this day. When I stepped outside and felt the warmth of the sun on my face, I was filled with gratitude. I don't always recognize my days as gifts. They can blur together into a string of indistinguishable moments. But I am learning to enjoy my life, bit by bit.

Lord, give me a desire for my own life. Help me exchange grumblings for peaceful prayers. May I always feel the warmth of Your light and celebrate each day fully.

What I Say I Want

I have no peace, no quietness;
I have no rest, but only turmoil.

JOB 3:26

"If only I could have some peace and quiet," I said
to a friend the other day. Yet in the evening when I have
a chance for serenity, I create distractions. God, why do
I set myself up for chaos? Maybe I'm afraid of spending
time alone with my thoughts and feelings.

I want to rest in You and lean into the quiet. Still
my thoughts and show me how to make quality time
for myself and for You. And the next time I wish for
the wonder of silence, I will actually know what I am
talking about.

When the World Sleeps

Those living far away fear your wonders;
where morning dawns and evening fades
you call forth songs of joy.

PSALM 65:8

Others are sleeping, and the night is filled with sounds of nocturnal life. Normally I would be frustrated about the lack of sleep, but tonight I like the tranquility. I like talking to You, knowing that You don't slumber but are with me every moment.

I can call out to You in the cave of night or the sky of day. Your omnipresence assures me at any hour. Before the dawn, the lullaby of Your voice is clear, and my spirit joins in.

Giving Over

*Submit to God and be at peace with him; in this
way prosperity will come to you. Accept instruction
from his mouth and lay up his words in your heart.*

JOB 22:21-22

I listen for Your instruction, Lord. I want to give
myself over to Your leading and Your will. Provide me
with a discerning heart so I do not listen to my own
wants but am attentive and open to Your desires for
my life.

Each word that comes from You is a gift to treasure, to store up, to use, and to follow. Break down
the walls I have built out of expectations and selfish
demands. I am ready to receive the peace of Your life-
giving wisdom.

Love

If Not Love

*If I have the gift of prophecy and can fathom all
mysteries and all knowledge, and if I have a faith
that can move mountains, but have not love, I am
nothing.*

1 CORINTHIANS 13:2

When my days are difficult or I face trials where
my own strength is useless, I know that I am held up
by You. It is not only my faith that ties me to You, but
it is Your love for me that gives me courage, hope, and
the perseverance required.

I draw encouragement from understanding my
gifts and my purpose in You, yet I know that these
do not shape me, make me, or sustain me. Only Your
love does that.

Empathy

For I wrote you out of great distress and anguish
of heart and with many tears, not to grieve you
but to let you know the depth of my love for you.

2 CORINTHIANS 2:4

Lord, grant me a portion of Your heart for others. I do not always know what needs a person has or what sorrows he or she holds inside. Give me Your eyes to notice such things. It is easy to distance myself from the hurt of a stranger or even the struggles of friends who do not speak out. Give me a love so deep that it forgives, it covers, it embraces, and it protects the people You bring into my life.

Insight

And this is my prayer: that your love may abound more and more in knowledge and depth of insight, so that you may be able to discern what is best and may be pure and blameless until the day of Christ.

PHILIPPIANS 1:9-10

I have a friend who has great instinct for what to do or what to say at any given moment. Meanwhile, I take a step back, afraid that I might do the wrong thing and make the situation worse. When does my faith lead to a sense of confidence?

Infuse me with courage and insight, Lord. I know it is my own insecurity that keeps me back in the shadows and holds me in a pattern of indecision. This also prevents me from demonstrating Your love and Your power to others in my life. Tomorrow, I will step out in faith in some way. It is time to live in Your knowledge with confidence.

Love Is

May your unfailing love rest upon us, O Lord,
even as we put our hope in you.

PSALM 33:22

Love is unfailing and uncompromising. Your love is a shining star in the night's sky that leads us forward and toward the hope of tomorrow. You know my steps before I ponder which way to go. You offer me free will so that I can choose to follow my Creator in love and submission.

I place my hope in You at all times. Help me to never invest myself and my faith in the things of the world.

Hope

Some Day

*But by faith we eagerly await through the Spirit
the righteousness for which we hope.*

GALATIANS 5:5

Flashbacks from the day produce images of me
making mistakes, missing opportunities, and sinning.
I hardly noticed the little white lies or the insensitivities
at the time. But I'm starting to become more aware of
these indiscretions. My faith is moving me toward righteousness, but it will be Your grace that gets me there.

I'm starting to believe there is hope for me yet.

Counting on You

I will praise you forever for what you have done;
in your name I will hope, for your name is good.

PSALM 52:9

When I speak of Your name and praise You for what You have given to me and brought me through, some people do not know how to respond. It makes them uncomfortable because they have not experienced the same. They have been let down by people; therefore, it is hard for them to imagine a God who does not fail, who does not leave.

I want to share hope in You. Grant me a gentle spirit and give me an understanding heart so that I might show Your goodness through my actions and my continued praise.

Pray It, Don't Say It

*Do not let this Book of the Law depart from your
mouth; meditate on it day and night, so that you
may be careful to do everything written in it. Then
you will be prosperous and successful.*

JOSHUA 1:8

My mouth has been eager to talk of Your mercy and
Your truth, but I am not good at meditating on Your
wisdom and Your law. I select bits of Your Word as I
need it to prove a point or to demonstrate my knowledge. How silly I can be. This is not serving You, and
it is not leading me to the purpose and prosperity You
long to give me.

Only when I own Your truths deep within my mind,
heart, and spirit can they produce fruit in my life. Only
when I commit to holding Your character in esteem
will I have the hope of becoming more like You.

Faithfulness

A longing fulfilled is sweet to the soul.

PROVERBS 13:19

God, You are so faithful to me. Your goodness surrounds me daily. I asked for help today, and You answered me in surprising ways. I felt vulnerable and needed a sense of protection and care—and You were there. I have longed for this kind of security all my life. Even with faith, I often doubted that You might be there to catch me should I fall.

But today I realized that the hunger is gone and fulfillment is in its place. You have met my longing with the sweetness of a future and a hope.

Nourishment

You Know Me

You understand, O Lord; remember me and care for me.

JEREMIAH 15:15

You see me when nobody else does. You know me when nobody else inquires. You see me when others look past me. You care for me when others are too busy. Being Your child means I am nourished spiritually and emotionally even when I feel alone.

How many times have I looked to others to feed me my sense of value? God, renew my strength and my understanding of how much You care. I am known by the Creator of the universe, and He loves me!

Strange Food

He humbled you, causing you to hunger and then feeding you with manna, which neither you nor your fathers had known, to teach you that man does not live on bread alone but on every word that comes from the mouth of the LORD.

DEUTERONOMY 8:3

I have begged for assistance and for You to ease my hunger, Lord. There is so much that I want. My journey is difficult at times, and I seek support. I have asked over and over for You to send answers and understanding and help.

Lord, all this time You have been providing me with all that I need. My concerns are understood. My path might not look like I want it to, but You are paving it with Your promises if only I would pay attention. Your Word and these promises are different than the food I asked for, but they nourish me and renew my spirit.

Casting Cares

Cast your cares on the LORD and he will sustain you.

PSALM 55:22

What do people do when they don't have You in their lives? I lay awake tonight wondering where I would be if I hadn't met You. I am blessed with strong relationships and friendships, yet not one person in my life could handle the cares and worries I entrust to You.

Not only do You hear my troubles, but You exchange them for what I need in that moment and for the long journey. People provide pat answers; You provide eternal promises. I am grateful to bring my whole heart to You.

Source of Life

You care for the land and water it; you enrich it abundantly.

PSALM 65:9

Showers cleanse the air. Sun warms the soil. Winds blow seeds across the land. Seasons set in motion by Your hand nourish the plants and the people and the generations of those who live beneath Your gaze.

My life feels like a complete system—a mini-world—that depends on Your cleansing grace, the warmth of Your compassion, and Your transforming love. Help me harvest the seeds You have planted in my soul. I know that abundance awaits me.

Completion

Here to There

*Perseverance must finish its work so that you may
be mature and complete, not lacking anything.*

JAMES 1:4

As my day comes to a close, I think about the large gap between where I am and where I want to be. I don't mean financially or professionally, but in the ways of faith. I want to know You more intimately and take Your precepts to heart.

Each day is a new opportunity to become more Christlike. Hold me accountable, Lord. Keep me in the company of those who will encourage and challenge me. Between here to there is a leap of faith, but I'm ready for the strides required.

Looking for the Line

*Now finish the work, so that your eager willing-
ness to do it may be matched by your completion
of it, according to your means.*

2 CORINTHIANS 8:11

My home is overrun with half-finished projects and
partially read books. I started and stopped four exer-
cise programs last year alone. So what makes me think
I can continue in my faith and complete the task of
growing in You? I don't know what the finish line will
look like, but I am watching for it. I am being perfected
in Your grace, and I am becoming more excited about
fulfilling Your purpose for my life.

The finish line is up ahead, and I know You are
shaping the twists and turns of my race to get me
there.

Reaching for the Baton

*I have fought the good fight, I have finished the
race, I have kept the faith.*

2 TIMOTHY 4:7

My pursuit of complete faith has become a relay.
Lord, You have given me so many prayer warriors,
encouragers, and godly examples to follow. Each one
of them provides me with a baton of wisdom and
the belief that I can go further. Now I eagerly watch
for the next lesson that will mold my view of what it
means to be Your child.

Past discouragements are completely out of view
and out of mind. I have kept the faith, and You, Lord,
have kept me fighting the good fight.

No More Settling

However, I consider my life worth nothing to me,
if only I may finish the race and complete the task
the Lord Jesus has given me—the task of testifying
to the gospel of God's grace.

ACTS 20:24

All I wanted to accomplish today was to survive. My plate was so full, and I felt overwhelmed. How often do I settle for such a limited view of my day's purpose? "I just want to get by" turns into "Where did last month go?" I'm caught in a faithless rut.

Lord, give me a deeper vision for tomorrow. The completion of one day is the continuation of a bigger plan. I pray my life will be a testimony to Your grace. Turn my limited goals into grander, eternal passions.

Silence

Hold My Tongue

If you have anything to say, answer me; speak up,
for I want you to be cleared. But if not, then listen
to me; be silent, and I will teach you wisdom.

JOB 33:32-33

God, I've never asked for this before, but I need to learn to be silent. You have placed wise people in my life who have advice and clear thinking to offer me. My pride gets in the way, and I pretend to know what I am doing. But I want to hear their truths. I want to be open to what You are teaching me through them.

Hold my tongue, open my ears, and prepare my heart for all You are saying to me.

Speaking with Actions

For it is God's will that by doing good you should silence the ignorant talk of foolish men.

1 PETER 2:15

As I think over the day, I realize there were many opportunities to express my beliefs through my actions. Lord, help me have a faith so real, so infused throughout my being that I do not have to rely just on words to express my love for You.

When I serve You by being compassionate, wise, generous, forgiving, and loving, those who want to undermine faith with false accusations or ignorant comments will be silenced, and those who long to know more about You will have a chance to "hear" the good news.

Tears

*O my God, I cry out by day, but you do not
answer, by night, and am not silent.*

PSALM 22:2

Lord, do You hear my cries? I am lonely. Nighttime
seems to echo with my sadness and even memories
of past disappointments. The distractions of daytime
seem so far away. I don't want to face this silence alone.
I want to hear from You; I want to be certain You are
right here beside me.

God listen to the brokenness of my spirit. I pray
for comfort as I sit in the silence and accept the balm
of Your presence.

Turning, Turning

*You turned my wailing into dancing; you removed
my sackcloth and clothed me with joy, that my
heart may sing to you and not be silent.*

PSALM 30:11-12

My time of weeping has ended. The grieving that
once consumed me has dissipated into the night. My
heart is turning toward joy and life. My feet are turning
as I dance into a new stage.

Oh, how I have waited for You to turn my sorrow
to celebration. My lips cannot stop praising You and
singing of Your goodness. I want to tell the world that
You walk with us through the pain and You rejoice
with us in our day of healing. Hallelujah!

Listening

My Mother Taught Me

He who answers before listening—that is his folly and his shame.

PROVERBS 18:13

During my childhood, I was sent to my room a few times for speaking out of turn. Usually I was trying to prove a point—a really good point, of course. Lord, I am not so different as an adult. I am eager to set the record straight. I don't even recognize this fault until it is too late and the words have been spoken.

Lord, convict me when my desire to clarify or correct is hindering a relationship, a conversation, a chance to listen with my whole heart.

What Catches My Attention

She had a sister called Mary, who sat at the Lord's feet listening to what he said. But Martha was distracted by all the preparations that had to be made.

LUKE 10:39-40

I worry about my well-being, about my security and future. There is much to be done in order to provide for tomorrow. Such thoughts consume me. You are here with me, and still my mind races with to-do lists, figures, and concerns. Lord, steer me from the distractions that plague me. I want to be the one who will drop anything and everything—my plans, my expectations, my will—to spend time at Your feet.

Following You begins with listening to You. Let me put aside my agenda and sit at Your feet all my days.

Answer Buffet

But as for me, I watch in hope for the LORD, I wait for God my Savior; my God will hear me.

MICAH 7:7

The world has many answers. My concerns seem ripe for the world's intervention. But I want my hope to be in You alone. I am trying not to listen to advice that is born of commercial pursuits and overeager self-help gurus. I let such guesses pass me by while I wait upon You and Your Word.

Hear me now, Lord. Do not let me wait in vain. My eyes are watching and my ears are listening for the Provider of hope and the final answers to all of life's questions.

Tonight

*Surely then you will find delight in the Almighty
and will lift up your face to God. You will pray to
him, and he will hear you, and you will fulfill your
vows.*

JOB 22:26-27

The time will come when I will face the night with
hope. There will be anticipation as I plan to tell You
all about my troubles and my heartaches. Right now I
am still overcome with my trials. I know You are here,
carrying me through them, but I have been reluctant
to listen to what You have to tell me.

Tonight I will lift up my face to You and step into
Your presence wholly.

Breathing

Ah...

How can I, your servant, talk with you, my lord?
My strength is gone and I can hardly breathe.

DANIEL 10:17

I can hear my own breathing. It is rough with fatigue after my long day. As much as I love this time to talk with You, I barely have the energy to put together a few thoughts. Breathing in and out reminds me of how intricately I am formed. There are so many ways in which You keep my life in motion, even when I don't have the strength.

Resting in Your presence feels good. Do You mind if I stay quiet? The pace of my breathing reminds me of Your heartbeat.

My Time

You have made my days a mere handbreadth;
the span of my years is as nothing before you.
Each man's life is but a breath.

PSALM 39:5

My focus is on my life. On what affects me. On what I need. On who I know. On how I live. My personal experiences become my foundation. This is all I know. But You who gave life to all of creation know that my time to taste, feel, laugh, cry, and pray is limited. You want me to live more fully. Lord, give me the capacity to love and feel and care with Your sensitivity and understanding. May my vision extend beyond my small world.

My life is but a breath. May I celebrate it.

In the Quiet

They were glad when it grew calm, and he guided them to their desired haven.

PSALM 107:30

Lead me to the stillness of this evening, God. Grant my heart the peace it longs for. A busy day feels good, but this time of quiet with You feels even better. Soothe the rapid beating of my heart. Lengthen and deepen my breaths so that I can rest and take in the gift of renewal.

I'm not good at letting go of the day, Lord. But tonight I give you my today and my tomorrow, and allow myself to surrender to this moment of quiet in Your arms.

How I Know

*But it is the spirit in a man, the breath of the
Almighty, that gives him understanding.*

JOB 32:8

People ask me how I can believe in You when
there is such hardship and trouble in the world. I don't
always provide a great answer. But I do know that I
could not make sense of the world if I didn't have faith
in a loving Creator.

In my spirit is Your breath, Your wisdom, and Your
presence, Lord. You give me understanding that goes
beyond head knowledge. You anchor me in faith with
Your love and Your mercy. This is how I know to trust
the way of faith.

All That I Have

May my prayer be set before you like incense;
may the lifting up of my hands be like
the evening sacrifice.

PSALM 141:2

It isn't much, this offering of my life, but it is all that I have to give. It isn't much, this day I have lived, but it is all that I know right now. My praise might not sound like the salutation of angels, but it is all my lips can form.

My heart is often empty, but it is ready to be filled by Your love. My future is uncertain, but it is Yours to shape. My prayer tonight is much like it is every night, but it is born of my spirit of gratitude. May You receive these humble offerings with pleasure and grace. Amen.

The One-Minute Prayers™ series